THE UNIVERSE

STARS

ABDO
Publishing Company

A Buddy Book by Fran Howard

VISIT US AT
www.abdopublishing.com

Published by ABDO Publishing Company, 8000 West 78th Street, Edina, Minnesota 55439.

Editor: Sarah Tieck
Contributing Editor: Michael P. Goecke
Graphic Design: Maria Hosley
Cover Image: Photos.com
Interior Images: Lushpix (page 11); NASA: Goddard Space Flight Center (page 15), Jet Propulsion Laboratory (page 17, 18), Johnson Space Center – Earth Sciences and Image Analysis (page 9), Kennedy Space Center (page 30); Photos.com (page 19, 25, 27, 29); Rich Reid (page 5).

Library of Congress Cataloging-in-Publication Data

Howard, Fran, 1953-
  Stars / Fran Howard.
    p. cm. — (The universe)
  Includes index.
  ISBN 978-1-59928-931-1
  1. Stars—Juvenile literature. I. Title.

QB801.7.H69 2008
523.8—dc22
                                    2007027787

Table Of Contents

What Is A Star?

At night, tiny lights dot the sky. These lights are stars.

Stars are glowing balls of gas that give off light. Thousands of them can be seen from Earth.

Most stars look very small and can only be seen at night. But, they are actually very large! Stars just look small because they are far away.

The sun is the closest star to Earth. Because it is so close, it appears large and bright in the daytime sky.

Special photography makes it possible to see the movement of stars over time.

A Closer Look

There are many different kinds of stars. Scientists group them based on size, mass, brightness, temperature, and color.

Most stars share a similar structure. At the center of a star is its core. The core is filled with gases, such as hydrogen and helium.

The core is the hottest part of the star. Heat and light move outward from the core toward the star's surface. But, the surface is much cooler than the core.

The chromosphere and the corona form a star's outer **atmosphere**. These layers are hotter than the star's surface.

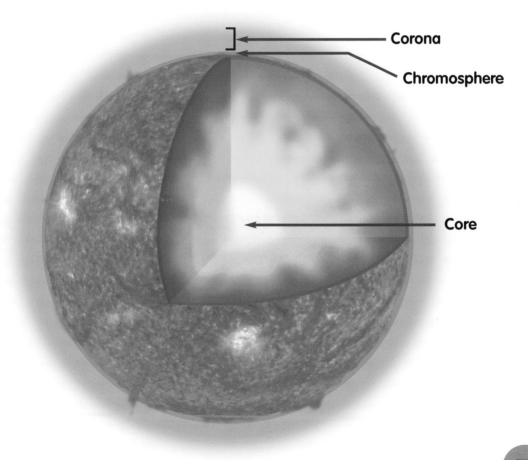

Corona

Chromosphere

Core

Beneath The Surface

Inside a star, hydrogen and helium react with each other. They get very hot and cause small **nuclear reactions**. These reactions create energy, which moves to the surface of the star. This causes the star to give off heat and light.

A star's color depends on the amount of heat on its surface. The hottest stars are blue. Other stars are white, yellow, orange, or red. A star can change color many times during its life cycle.

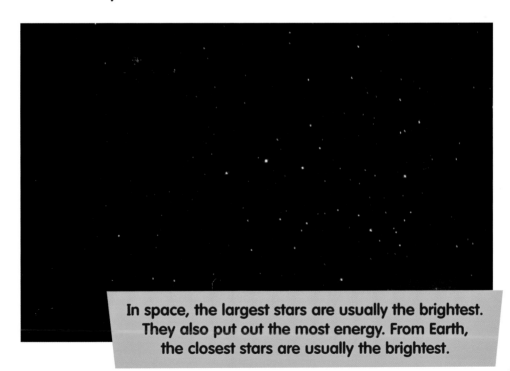

In space, the largest stars are usually the brightest. They also put out the most energy. From Earth, the closest stars are usually the brightest.

A Star Is Born

A star begins as a cloud of gas. As the cloud rotates, heat and pressure build. The mass begins to **collapse** on itself. At 20 million degrees Fahrenheit (11 million °C), **nuclear reactions** occur. A star is born!

The cloud that a star forms in is called a nebula.

The Life Of A Star

Often, scientists can tell a star's age by its size. For example, our sun is a dwarf star.

Dwarf stars are medium-sized stars. Stars usually stay in the dwarf stage until they begin to run out of fuel.

The surface temperature and brightness of dwarf stars increase with age. As they begin to use up their energy, dwarf stars become red giant stars.

Red giants can be about 1,000 times bigger than dwarf stars. They are also cooler. When a red giant uses up its energy, it becomes a white dwarf.

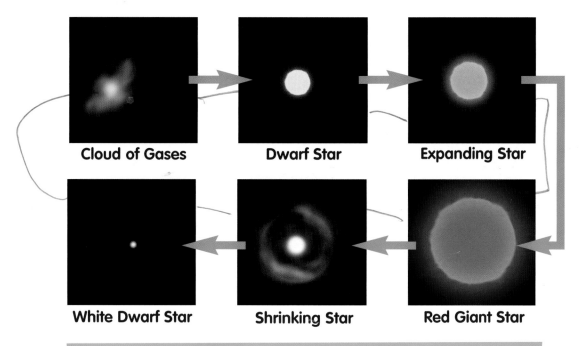

Cloud of Gases	Dwarf Star	Expanding Star
White Dwarf Star	Shrinking Star	Red Giant Star

As stars change, there are some in-between stages. Dwarf stars grow larger as they turn into red giants. Red giants form clouds of dust and gas as they become white dwarfs.

Supergiants are the biggest known stars in our **galaxy**. They can be hundreds of times bigger than our sun. Supergiants are also much brighter. However, supergiants do not live as long as smaller stars.

In our galaxy, there are stars in each stage of life.

The Death Of A Star

At the end of their lives, stars go through many changes. Some stars get bigger as they age. Others change color.

Many aging stars **collapse**. This happens when a star runs out of fuel to burn. Then, the star's center falls in on itself.

Some large stars explode. This explosion sends pieces of the stars into space.

White dwarf stars are dying stars. They become smaller as they run out of fuel.

Our Galaxy

Groups of stars form **galaxies**. A small galaxy has about 10 million stars. A large galaxy may have up to 1 trillion stars!

Our galaxy is called the Milky Way. It is a large galaxy. Our sun is one of many stars in the Milky Way.

The Milky Way is spiral shaped.

There are at least 200 billion stars in the Milky Way. Yet, only about 6,000 of them can be seen from Earth without a telescope.

Our **galaxy** is filled with solar systems. A solar system is a single star with space objects, such as planets, orbiting it.

Our sun is at the center of our solar system. Earth is one of eight planets that orbit our sun. The other planets are Mercury, Venus, Mars, Jupiter, Saturn, Uranus, and Neptune.

The sun is the only star in our solar system. But, it is one of 200 billion stars in our galaxy. Some scientists think our galaxy may have as many as 400 billion stars!

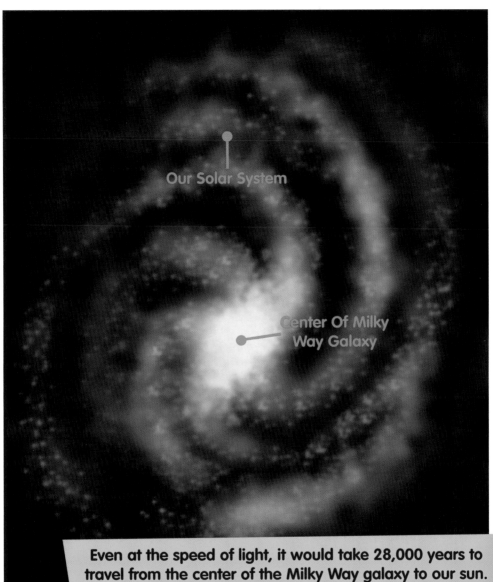

Our Solar System

Center Of Milky
Way Galaxy

Even at the speed of light, it would take 28,000 years to travel from the center of the Milky Way galaxy to our sun.

Discovering Stars

For thousands of years, poets, farmers, and astronomers have named the many patterns in the night sky. These patterns are called constellations. Today, there are 88 official constellations.

Constellations help people map the sky. People use them to find particular stars. Also, astronomers use them as markers to point to other stars.

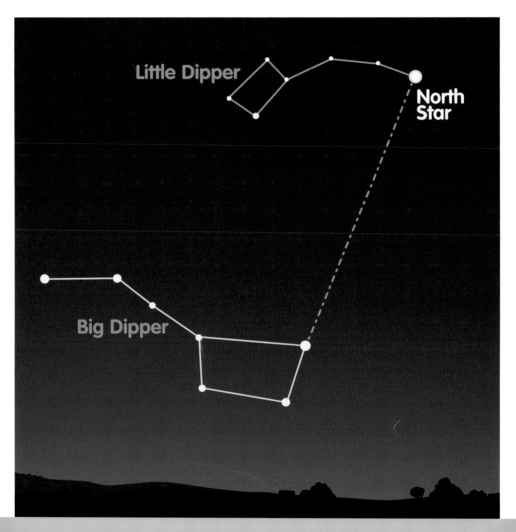

The North Star can be found by locating the Big Dipper constellation. Simply draw a line through the two stars that form the end of the Big Dipper's bowl. These stars are called pointer stars. They point to the first star in the Little Dipper's handle. This is the North Star.

In the 1800s, scientists began measuring the distance from Earth to stars. In 1896, U.S. astronomer Annie Cannon began placing stars in groups. She based the groups on temperature. This was the beginning of modern star groupings.

More recently, scientists have learned about the life cycles of stars. They have continued to discover new stars, too.

In the late 1700s, British astronomer William Herschel made a discovery. He found that two or more stars can orbit one center together.

Missions To The Stars

The first **spacecraft** to be sent to a star were *Pioneer 6, 7, 8,* and *9*. The United States **launched** these **probes** in the 1960s to orbit the sun.

These missions allowed scientists to learn more about the sun and other stars. In 2007, scientists thought some of these probes were still orbiting.

Scientists also use powerful telescopes to learn about stars. Some telescopes are in space. Others are on Earth.

Space-based telescopes lie outside Earth's atmosphere. This allows them to get more detailed images of distant space objects such as stars.

Fact Trek

In space, distance is measured in light-years and light-minutes. One light-year describes how far light travels in one year. This is very far. Light travels nearly 6 trillion miles (10 trillion km) in a year!

Think about how fast light fills a room when you flick a switch!

Another name for the North Star is Polaris.

Ancient astronomers once believed that the stars were fixed in the sky. But today, scientists know that stars move.

People have observed the stars for thousands of years.

The sun is about eight light-minutes from Earth. Proxima Centauri is the second-closest star to Earth. It is about four light-years away.

Voyage To Tomorrow

People are continuing to explore space. They want to learn more about stars.

Scientists use very powerful telescopes to study groups of stars. This helps them learn about the life cycles of stars and **galaxies**.

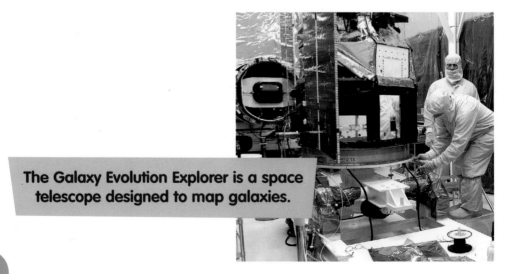

The Galaxy Evolution Explorer is a space telescope designed to map galaxies.

Important Words

atmosphere the layer of gases that surrounds space objects, including planets, moons, and stars.

collapse to break down.

galaxy a large group of stars and planets.

launch to send off with force.

mission the sending of spacecraft to perform specific jobs.

nuclear reaction a change in matter that creates energy.

probe a spacecraft that attempts to gather information.

spacecraft a vehicle that travels in space.

Web Sites

To learn more about **stars**, visit ABDO Publishing Company on the World Wide Web. Web sites about **stars** are featured on our Book Links page. These links are routinely monitored and updated to provide the most current information available.

www.abdopublishing.com

INDEX